FREUD

AND

ME

MICHELE BAKER, M.D.
LAURA CRAIN, M.D.
KATHRYN V. JONES, M.D.
MARY McCARTHY, M.D.
CRIS RATINER, Ph.D.

PHILLIP FREEMAN, M.D., D.M.H.
ANTON KRIS, M.D.
ANNA ORNSTEIN, M.D.
CORDELIA SCHMIDT-HELLERAU, Ph.D.
STEPHEN STERNBACH, M.D.

Editors:
DAN JACOBS, M.D.
STEVEN MORANDI

CONTENTS

ACKNOWLEDGEMENTS

It is a privilege to bring forth this tribute to Sigmund Freud on the 150th anniversary of his birth. This publication, however goes beyond honoring Freud. It also celebrates our life as a community of clinicians and scholars at the Boston Psychoanalytic Society and Institute. We are indebted to Phillip Freeman for first suggesting to the Faculty Executive Committee that a "Freud and Me" symposium be held with candidates from each academic year participating, and to Patricia Wright and Jack Beinashowitz, who extended the discussion to include faculty at the Members Meeting they organized. Jonathan Palmer's painting reproduced on the cover of this volume was a gift from him to our Institute. The administrative staff at BPSI— Diana Nugent, Beth Jordan, and Karen Smolens— facilitated the production of this book in many ways. Lastly we wish to thank the Hanns Sachs Library Committee—William Ackerly, Renée Gelman, Sanford Gifford, Merna Lipsitt, David Mobley, Rae Silberger, and Anna Wolff—for the commitment of funds from their budget that makes this publication possible.

Dan Jacobs, M.D.
Steven Morandi

CONTRIBUTORS

Michele Baker was born in Boston at Beth Israel Hospital where she now works as an inpatient psychiatrist and in a private outpatient practice. In between she attended college and medical school in New England, venturing as far as New Haven where she met her husband who is in Rabbinical school. The two of them have two sons: Samson and Moses, and live all together with the dog in a tiny Brookline Village abode.

Laura Crain is a fifth year candidate at the Boston Psychoanalytic Society and Institute. She has been in full time private psychiatric practice since 1990, and currently practices in Back Bay, Boston. She is a faculty member of the Massachusetts General Hospital Center for Group Psychotherapy, where she supervises and teaches psychiatry residents. She gratefully acknowledges her husband and two sons, as well as her colleagues, psychoanalyst, supervisors and teachers, for bringing Freud to life.

Phillip Freeman is a Training and Supervising psychoanalyst at the Boston Psychoanalytic Society and Institute with a private practice in Newton. He recently completed a term as Chair of the Joint Curriculum Committee and Faculty Executive Committee. He served as moderator for the "Freud and Me" academic lecture.

Daniel Jacobs is a Training and Supervising Analyst at the Boston Psychoanalytic Society and Institute and Supervising Analyst at the Florida and Cincinnati Psychoanalytic Institutes. He is director of the Hanns Sachs Library.

Anton Kris is a practicing psychoanalyst and a Training and Supervising Analyst and faculty member at the Boston Psychoanalytic Society and Institute. He is also a Clinical Professor of Psychiatry at Harvard Medical School.

Kathryn Jones is a candidate at the Boston Psychoanalytic Society and Institute. She has been a teacher in the Cambridge Hospital child psychiatry program and the Harvard Longwood Psychiatry Residency. A Toronto native, she is in private practice in Brookline, MA.

Mary McCarthy has a private practice in Brookline, MA and is on the faculty at the Brigham and Women's Hospital where formerly she was the Training Director for 10 years. She recently learned from a patient that the reputed quote of Freud's about the Irish was spoken by Jack Nicholson in the current movie, *The Departed*. That quote is getting around!

Steven Morandi is the librarian of the Hanns Sachs Library at the Boston Psychoanalytic Society and Institute. Currently, he is also finishing his Ph.D. in archaeology at Boston University.

Anna Ornstein is Professor Emerita of Child Psychiatry at the University of Cincinnati and currently is a Supervising Analyst at the Boston Psychoanalytic Society and Institute.

Jonathan Palmer is a Training and Supervising Analyst at the Boston Psychoanalytic Society and Institute.

Cris Ratiner is a child clinical psychologist who has alternated between outpatient private practice, community mental health care and humanitarian relief efforts in the developing world. Most recently she served as psychosocial consultant to UNICEF following the Pakistan earthquake of October 2005. She received her Ph.D. from Boston University and her Master's degree in public administration from the Kennedy School of Government.

Cordelia Schmidt-Hellerau has studied and trained in Switzerland where she is a Training and Supervising Analyst and a Permanent Lecturer for Clinical Psychology with Special Emphasis on Psychoanalysis at the University of Zurich. She has published two books and numerous articles on psychoanalytic theory and its clinical applications. In Boston since 2000, she is a member of the faculty at the three Psychoanalytic Institutes, BPSI, PINE and MIP, and has been teaching various courses, in particular on Freud. In 2006 she was appointed a Training and Supervising Analyst at the Boston Psychoanalytic Society and Institute. She is working in private practice in Chestnut Hill, MA.

Stephen Sternbach is on the faculty of Boston Psychoanalytic Society and Institute. He has participated in panel discussions and written about psychoanalytic issues from both Freudian and Lacanian perspectives.

PHILLIP FREEMAN

Introduction

Despite and, perhaps, in consequence of theoretical pluralism, psychoanalysis remains dominated by the voice of its founder. Extolled and resented in generational dramas best understood by the very theories that bear his name, Sigmund Freud looms large.

Some say "too large". They argue that, just as geneticists no longer study Mendel, it is past time that Freud's works be rendered historical curiosities. And yet, year after year, faculty and trainees discover the excitement and value of encountering and learning from that voice.

As the 150th anniversary of Freud's birth approached, the members of the BPSI Curriculum Committee chose a format for an institute-wide presentation that they hoped would capture the spirit of the very personal encounter with the writings of Sigmund Freud that is so central to the developing professional identity of every psychoanalyst. Five candidates, one from each seminar year, agreed to tell their stories. The talks were intended to be informal but to read them is to be impressed by the psychoanalytic themes—symbolism and dream work, infantile longings and modes of thought, conflict and the role of the past, repetition and transference to name a few—that demonstrate the continuing influence and utility of Freud's ideas.

The candidates' meetings with Freud are personal. They are recounted from particular vantage points and offer particular concerns. Michele Baker approaches Freud by way of their shared skepticism about religion. She deftly considers how Freud's positions might require modification in her own "post-mechanical" day. She hears a note of faith in contemporary arguments for unconscious mental functioning. She detects rationalism in the move away from a personalized deity. She argues that the convergence

1

of religious belief and psychoanalysis undercuts Freud's "clean division" between the rational and the illusory.

Kate Jones approaches Freud, she says, by way of the drives. She flirts, plays, and grapples with that "particular long shadow." She considers Freud as a man, a male authority, a foreigner, and a visitor from "across time." She speculates that her, and our, difficulties fully integrating or mourning Freud may be due, in part, to theories intentionally constructed to secure his legacy: the primal Father that grows larger in death.

Cris Ratiner approaches Freud by way of caricatures of Freud in film and TV. She feels protective. When she re-encounters Freud incarnated in her mentors, she is alerted to a pull towards idealization. Mary McCarthy approaches Freud by way of her self-described resistances. As she develops her psychoanalytic ear for the symbolic, she longs to meet a Freud who will appreciate what she has learned. In gratitude, she offers a loving appreciation for what she has received.

Laura Crain approaches Freud as an ambivalently received visitor into her family life. Time must be sacrificed and space must be made. She observes and interprets representations of the intrusion in the creative play of her children. She returns to the question of Freud on religion introduced by Baker, only here the accent is on the danger, perhaps the excitement, of forbidden, heretical knowledge.

Some weeks after the candidate "Freud and Me" presentations, three members of the faculty—Stephen Sternbach, Cordelia Schmidt-Hellerau, and Anna Ornstein—were invited to offer talks on a similar theme. The faculty members admitted that their talks were, perhaps inevitably, less personal, but their scholarly contributions, whether they accented an elaboration of Freud, a tangent, or a cross current, continued to demonstrate the centrality of Freud as a point of departure.

On the night of the faculty presentations, Tony Kris showed a film that his mother, Marianne Kris, shot in 1956 at Freud's London home on the occasion of the 100th anniversary of Freud's birth, seventeen years after his death. Present were a collection of analysts for whom the "Freud and Me" title would have been less ironic and more literal. While it is interesting to speculate about the impact of real versus imagined encounters with the author, it is evident both from the immediate, vital engagements described by the candidates, and from the more down-stream contributions of the faculty, that, far from an "historical curiosity", is the curiosity that the encounter with Freud remains so fresh.

MARY McCARTHY

A Birthday Letter to Freud

Dear Freud:

Happy Birthday! Whenever you write a Birthday greeting, it requires a review of what the person means to you, and frequently involves best wishes for health, love, prosperity and the like. Since you've been dead 67 years or so, only the former task applies. This year, my class has traversed your writings on sex, aggression, God, religion, the role of the father and the formation of laws and civilization. In "Totem and Taboo", you introduced us to the primal horde composed of the dominant male who had easy access to the females, causing envy and homicidal rage in the other males, the sons, leading them to kill the primal father which led to remorse, terrible guilt and ultimately the formation of laws and institutions, what we call civilization. We struggled with the concepts of the death instinct, libido, aggression, the pleasure principle, ambivalence and love. Despite the fact that I've known about you and read some of your works before, this year especially, you have really gotten to me. There has been a taking in of you, an identification, an introjection that I am amazed by. I kept my distance in the past, appreciating your genius, but, preferring to think of you as having little to offer me. I was put-off and even angry about your theories of female development and your renunciation of the seduction hypothesis of neurosis which feels like throwing the baby out with the bathwater and has certainly caused a lasting backlash against psychoanalysis. I'm still in disagreement with your views on female psychology as are a good many people, but now I see it more as evidence of your human fallibility for which I breathe a sigh of relief. So you're wrong about some things. But how I've come to

5

appreciate your brilliance, your amazing insight into human
nature, your energy, and your incredible productivity!   I
find references to you, to psychoanalysis, and to your theories daily. Our culture has embraced your theories in such
a way that it has forgotten that these ideas came from you;
they are so automatic and deeply held. So, for a man who
did not believe in God or an afterlife, if this isn't an afterlife, what is?

Last summer on the way to a vacation in Ireland, I
found a reference to you in the *Aer Lingus* magazine.
There, in an article entitled "Do you Speak Irish?", the
writer attempted to explain the Irish sport of conversation
where the truth is less important than the wish to laugh
and be entertained. The writer went on to say that this can
be a problem when the Irish seek professional help. He
attributes to you the following quote "This is one race of
people for whom psychoanalysis is of no use whatsoever"
because you believed supposedly that the Irish couldn't tell
the difference between the truth and a good story. So this
is why my analysis is taking so long! This is almost certainly an apocryphal story since Steve, our librarian, could
find no reputable reference to it. But secretly I was tickled
by it, by the thought that you might have given any
thought to "my race of people" because, seriously, it can
feel a long way from the consulting rooms of Vienna to my
parents' tiny living room in Philadelphia where I grew up.

I've thought about how much I'd love to have met you
and felt your direct presence. Who among us hasn't entertained this thought? That we'd be a friend of yours, perhaps in your inner circle, a confidante, and that you'd see
in us even a tiny approximation of your brilliance; and that
recognition in your eyes would be enough. Or perhaps,
we'd be one of the rebels, taking you to task on some of
your thoughts, but preferring to remain in your good
graces, or taking it further and killing you off, metaphori-
cally speaking, by attacking and finally breaking away from
you. In any case, to have known you, I imagine, would
have been a defining moment in life. And to have been

able to tell you a clinical vignette like this:

One of my patients, a 40-year-old thrice-divorced man, is terribly conflicted around sexuality and enraged with women. He appears to have been over-stimulated sexually by his mother during latency with subsequent attempts to atone for his guilt at puberty with strict hand-washing rituals. He has been able to remain faithful to his current girlfriend but has been sorely tempted by a woman at work with whom he has developed a strong friendship but with whom he has not acted on any of his sexual feelings. Recently they were in a bar, where he noticed a woman nearby staring at him. He is a good-looking man and when his friend got up to go to the bathroom this woman leaned over, and said, "You're very handsome." My patient, a bit flustered, didn't quite know what to say. He finally replied without a trace of irony, "Well, I like your pocketbook." I imagine you might have chuckled, recognizing the sexual wish in the statement, recognizing another confirmation of your theory of the symbolic unconscious. What I am most amazed is that I hear it that way, too, now that my own resistance to unconscious realities has been breaking down, through the influences of our lectures, reading, my own analysis, and by doing analysis with my patients. I mean, a pocketbook is no longer just a pocketbook, to the consternation at times of my family and friends!

Now, let's move on to envy. According to you, all women suffer to some extent from penis envy. So much so, that in "On Transformation of Instinct As Exemplified in Anal Erotism" (Freud 1917), you wrote that a normal woman changes her wish for a penis to a wish for a man and "thus puts up with the man as an appendage to the penis." This statement is so deliciously provocative, in part, because it manages to offend both sexes at once! But that's not what I want to necessarily address here. What I want to talk about is how hard it is for women to find the kernels of truth in your writings about us because you had this tendency to make these incredibly troublesome statements. Let me tell you about this study recently done on

62 three- and four-year old children. Being a scientist at
heart, you'll appreciate this. Dr. Nancie Senet published
this in *The Psychoanalytic Quarterly* in 2004 (Senet 2004).
These children, all of whom knew their own gender identity, were asked to construct both a girl and a boy doll using any of an assortment of anatomical features including
both male and female genitals. 37% of the girls and 41%
of the boys included both set of genitals when making the
girl doll. 27% of the girls and 47% of boys did so when
constructing the boy doll. In other words, Freud, both
sexes are reluctant to give up claim to the other's genitals;
each envies the genitals of the opposite sex. You were
half-right. So, as I entertain the notion of penis envy in
my female patients, I begin to hear possible allusions to it:

The patient, a woman who just turned 40, childless and
without a romantic relationship, also feels unfulfilled in
her career. I have heard her say over and over again that
she feels she is missing something. A few months ago, she
was talking about feeling "stuck" with her mother, a mean,
unfulfilled, narcissistic woman, whose husband punished
her for going back to work by not speaking to her for a
year and never slept in the same room with her again.
During a session, the patient stated, "She affected me so
much that I feel mutilated, not whole." She went on to
worry that she *is* her mother in some way and will never
escape her. Again, she lamented that she felt mutilated,
"wounded." There was a way she said these words that
conveyed a deep pain, like a hurt animal. She talked about
how her mother taught her to be skeptical of being a
woman, to such an extent that the patient feels surprised
when people refer to her as a woman.

She is a woman who allows herself very few outward
touches of femininity. She buys a Chanel jacket and lets it
sit in her closet for years before finally giving it away. How
sad is that? So when I hear her carefully and painfully saying that she doesn't have what it takes, that she feels mutilated, and is missing something, I do think of your theory
that some women long for a penis. Is that what this

woman is trying to express, that "stuck" with her female body, she feels mutilated, wounded, without a penis? Perhaps, on some level, yes. Is she saying that her mother, in her intense ambivalence about being female and her anger at men wounded the patient's sense of primary femininity? Almost certainly, yes. That in being born male, she would have escaped the less preferential state of being a woman in her family and therefore would have felt more valued and loved? Probably yes. It goes on, but I do now consider envy of the male organ one possible unconscious source of her feelings.

This year in our Freud class, we read "Totem and Taboo" (Freud 1912-1913) and "Civilization and its Discontents" (Freud 1930[1929]). I found these texts powerful for many reasons. To me, you were trying to understand the essential bedrock conflicts of being human. A few years ago, one of my daughters, at about the age of seven or eight, protested vigorously during a discussion of evolution that there was no way that she was descended from an ape, absolutely no way. It offended her developing self deeply to consider that she is an animal. I think this basic fact continues to be one of the hardest things for each of us to contend with. I have come to see the animal instincts of aggression and sexuality as important motivators of behavior that have to be grappled with in any theory of the mind. In "Civilization and its Discontents" (Freud 1930[1929]), you enumerated the three sources of unhappiness in life: Our bodies—their decay and dissolution, Nature and its overwhelming destructiveness, and our relationships with each other. We have made progress with each of these areas, although all continue to humble us. In the fall, I visited the Holocaust Museum again. This time, I really saw you. There you were in a photo arriving in Paris after leaving your beloved Vienna, being supported by Anna, looking frail, with white hair and beard, perhaps feeling stunned and confused, even scared, at that moment. The forces that were unleashed in the world at that point were tremendously destructive, violent and hateful. It must have been terrifying to have been so right about human nature and so disorienting to have to leave your beloved home at that point in your life. But, I want you to know this: your work has not been in vain. You have given us a powerful tool to help our patients understand themselves, to help the world understand itself, and even though the world is not usually paying attention, you have had a far-reaching impact.

Thank you, and Happy Birthday, Dear Freud.

References

Freud, S. (1912-1913) Totem and Taboo. *Standard Edition*, Volume 13.

Freud, S. (1917) On Transformations of Instinct as Exemplified in Anal Erotism. *Standard Edition*, Volume 17.

Freud, S. (1930[1929]) Civilization and its Discontents. *Standard Edition*, Volume 21.

Senet, N. (2004) A Study of Preschool Children's Linking of Genitals and Gender. *Psychoanalytic Quarterly* 73:291-334.

KATHRYN V. JONES

Well here I am, ready for my 10 minutes with Freud. Me and the father of psychoanalysis, all alone... Well, hardly. Or should I invoke the other drive: ten minutes in the ring with Freud. I initially envisioned this talk as a delightful and friendly chat, perhaps with a cup of coffee in our hands—I am certainly no smoker of cigars. As time went by, it became an increasingly daunting task. Almost equal billing with Freud. "Freud and Me". I would hope I could hold my own with someone long departed. But he casts a long shadow, and it is an unfair match. The 21st century analyst grappling with that particular long shadow: this is my subject today.

Why all this intimidation regarding Freud? The answer to that, in part, lies in the private domain of our analyses but another part, I believe, involves an experience shared with many others. First, there is the fact of Freud's legacy. Writer of our book of genesis, he was a complicated man, a politically powerful man. He, like us all, had many selves, constantly in conflict and in evolution over his long life and he, unlike most of us, documented his mind and its working extensively. We know him mostly through his vivid writings that are full of a sense of personality.

Secondly, there is the need to contend with the depth and agility of his ever-active mind, the intellectual equivalent of the 12-marathon-a-year runner. In all there is, for the newly initiated, an experience, in the words of my colleague, Lisa Price, akin to that of "a child hearing classical music or tasting wine or hearing an opera. Much as these things can become quite pleasurable, it takes a lot of exposure".

And yet, despite tell-all academic treatises that purport to reveal Freud's human side with patients, his is a chamber not readily entered these days, even by the experienced. There is the image of the stern Freud, captured in innumerable photographs, and also in the melancholy portrait in our front hall (by the talented Jonathan Palmer), fixing us with his imposing and unafraid stare, radiating authority—male authority. He is superego personified, he sees and knows all and threatens to have the last word.

Also, there is an essential foreignness that is not easy to access. There is the matter of the layer of the dust of history that lies over his words. They come to us translated from another language, across time and from another social reality. The words themselves are a dense concoction of formality and wit, delightful yet distant in affect tone and not clinically experience-near. His patients are not really like our patients. The women he treats are constricted by historical roles mistakenly seen as psychological reality.

And why this ongoing powerful transference? Why is Freud larger than most deceased gifted thinkers? There remains an ongoing fascination with the works of Freud certainly well beyond our institution. A search by name on Google Scholar that holds a database of scholarly articles and books that Steve Morandi, the BPSI librarian, kindly obtained for me, reveals that hits to Freud are way up on the list, second to Einstein, getting more hits than Shakespeare and Darwin, and 300,000 more than Plato. Also, we often refer to Freud in the present tense. This interesting slip, I would offer, reveals some kind of unresolved mourning, a holding onto him as if he were still with us, 67 years after his death in September 1939.

There is this disparity in the largeness of his image and the reality of not actually knowing him. The humanizing and integrating that occurs with person to person contact with an ambivalently held object, can never occur with Freud. How often we are surprised at ourselves as we feel fondness in the presence of someone we had decided we were unsure of, in whose absence we had focused on his or her negative attributes. In being with the real person with the real smile and the real heartbeat, we take in their wholeness and we can add compassion and appreciation to the mix of feelings for that person.

What does it mean if our feelings for Freud are silent and unnoticed or not fully analyzed? He is like a father who died either early in some of our childhoods or before we were born. This seems a resemblance to certain types of mourning, particularly, mourning a parent we never knew or of whom there is only a handful of memories that fills in our internal representation of that lost object. For to me, there appears to be a paradox: our increasing freedom to think beyond Freud's beliefs, yet the existence of his quietly looming presence, the shadow of his object over our professional egos. As Jim Herzog has recently reminded me, in "Totem and Taboo" Freud (1912-1913) writes, "The father was even more powerful dead than alive".

Has Freud become to some a kind of psychoanalytic Obi Wan Kenobi from *Star Wars*, the great Jedi Knight who in death can exist psychically more and be more present with his apprentice, Luke Skywalker?

There are ingredients missing in our experience of Freud that preclude an integrated metabolizing of Freud and a balancing of conflicting transferences. Perhaps we need to take in more of his humanity and allow for more of our sympathetic affects in the mix. I know for me there is a wish to temper his sternness and his melancholy, for my own reasons. I wish to see a small smile upon his face. I imagine, what I have come to amuse myself by calling the image of the "Freud-alisa", Freud with a mysterious yet still world-weary smile. I will paint it for you with a couple of anecdotes.

This April in the *New York Times Magazine*, Mark Edmunson (2006) wrote an article entitled "Freud and the Fundamentalist Urge" that I am sure a number of you saw. The article does a service to Freud and to psychoanalysis and ultimately promotes a socially conscious message to "know thyself". It is well worth reading and time precludes me saying more about it other than to quote a description it contained of Freud's encounter with the Nazis that I found tremendously satisfying to read. "On the day after Hitler arrived in Vienna, a gang of Nazis stormed into Freud's apartment at 19 Bergasse. They ransacked the place and made off with a fairly large sum of money. ("I never got so much for a single session" Freud, never at a loss, observed.) They only left it is said, when the old man, trembling and frail, appeared from out of his consulting room and fixed them in his long-practiced stare. The Nazis, the story continues, scrambled for the door." That stern stare, now relentlessly inculcated within our shared psychoanalytic memory of Freud, shows him as able to fend off the Storm Troopers with one look, and leaves us wanting for similar powers in face of our worry—described so articulately by Phillip Freeman during his commencement address this past spring—of our own "obsolescence".

There is another wonderful example of Freud's sense of humor described by Ernst Jones in a 1940 tribute a few months after Freud's death. It is really a postscript to the story above. Taking place in the final chapters of his life, fleeing Vienna and welcomed by England, Jones recounts the moment the cancer-ridden Freud first sees the garden in Hampstead. Jones writes, "I shall never forget his humorously exultant cry of "Heil Hitler" when Freud first caught sight of the garden, where thanks to that baleful spirit, he was to enjoy many happy hours." (Jones 1957)

As I notice my urge to enliven Freud and make him an object with whom one can be more playful, two images come to mind. One is that of a photo which graces the cover of a recent novel called *Seduction* by a Canadian psychologist Catherine Gildiner (a murder mystery involving Da Vinci Code-esque Freudian intrigue): an archival photo I had never before seen of a smiling Freud with a smiling daughter Anna hiking in the Alps, on her way to shaping the future of child analysis. The other is the small gray Freud doll, or action figure, complete with cigar and frown; *de rigueur* in certain analytic offices, sometimes the gift of a patient seeking a way to alter or play with a perceived analytic stance. Recently, one of my daughters, having played with the Freud doll, announced, unprompted, "Freud is too serious. So I put purple polka dots all over him".

Plato wrote of five different forms of immortality including through the written word. By this yardstick and by many others, Freud has achieved immortality. As he aged, he increasingly focused on the development of theory centering around the Father in the larger sociological and anthropological context. Placing the father at the foreground of his theories, did he intentionally build himself into his theories and presage his historical importance? Undoubtedly his wife, and mother of his six children, had she a moment to cultivate theories would have constructed a different model of the mind. Perhaps one that involved a centrality of feeding and cleaning and healing and garden and earth metaphors.

Thank God Freud existed to unflinchingly cast his eye on such difficult, hard-to-take areas as human aggression, the repetition of our unconscious motives and the tangles into which they lead us. For the next 150 years, I hope that for us as analysts we can move forward in a balanced and nuanced way, that we can take in the Freud who could fashion humorous off-the-cuff remarks in the face of terrible events and delight with his daughter in the emergence of flowers on a mountainside.

References

Edmunson, M. (2006) Freud and the Fundamentalist Urge. *New York Times Magazine*. April 30.

Jones, E. (1957) *The Life and Work of Sigmund Freud*, Volume 3. New York: Basic Books, Inc.

Gildiner, C. (2005) *Seduction*. Vintage Canada.

MICHELE BAKER

Freud and Me: Two Godless Jews

Like many of you, I am Jewish. Like many of you I am an atheist. Luckily, I am in good company—Sigmund Freud was, like me, a Jewish atheist. Freud considered religiously oriented people to be resting in the arms of a delusion. For Freud, religion is a cultural obsessional neurosis in which the wish we all feel for someone who will take care of us is projected out into the universe. Freud wrote "religion is an attempt to master the sensory world in which we are situated by means of the wishful world which we have developed within us as a result of biological and psychological necessities. But religion cannot achieve this. Its doctrines bear the imprint of the times in which they arose, the ignorant times of the childhood of humanity. Its consolations deserve no trust" (Freud 1933[1932]: 168). In contrast to religion based on wishes, Freud's science of psychoanalysis was to be based upon truth—*scientific* truth, not upon meshugina ideas, which no matter how lovely and consoling, were unprovable. Just as enlightened individuals must give up the illusion of an omniscient God, so the patient on the couch was not to be gratified with support, but allowed only the bracing tonic of insight and interpretation.

I have focused my musings on the topic of "Freud and Me" on a current living tension in my life: between psychoanalysis and religion. At home I'm the atheist doctor and my husband Jim is the believer, studying to be a rabbi. As a future Rebbetzin (the special title for the wife of a rabbi) with two young children, I'm often in the position to grapple with religion—like it or not. There's nothing like a four-year-old to pierce one's most carefully crafted atheist-consistent yet God-friendly compromises. Last month my son asked me "What is God?" I answered:

"God is the idea people have of all the goodness in the world." He pointed up. "God is in the sky," he informed me.

So, just how different is what Jim does from what I do? Probably our practices are more alike than they would have been in Freud's time. Even the issue of belief may be a bugaboo: Jim sometimes accuses me of *believing* in the unconscious. Although for me, and I am quoting Tony Kris here, the idea of "unconscious" represents a useful, essential hypothesis, not a subject of belief. I see what we call the unconscious during my work, and in my life, in the shadow it casts, like the x-ray crystallography which helped crack the code of DNA. But, I admit, religious people see the work of God, perhaps with no less evidence. Unlike Freud who lived in a more mechanistic age and who believed that the scientific method would prove the tenets of psychoanalysis to be irrevocably true, I admit psychoanalysis feels, at least in part, faith-based. It seems to me that there have been two tectonic shifts in the past 75 years: religion has changed and psychoanalysis has changed. Perhaps they have each influenced each other and certainly our modern world has affected both. Neither seems to be practiced with the same level of orthodoxy which made Freud see them as irreconcilable.

In *Seek My Face: A Jewish Mystical Theology*, Arthur Green writes: "the faith in a transcendent and personal God, no longer satisfies our religious needs. The parental, royal, and pastoral metaphors we have inherited, beloved as they are, are not adequate for describing the relationship between God and world as we experience and understand it" (Green 2003:14). He goes on to describe, in words I can't do justice to here, a mystical breaking down of a God to whom people pray: "the self who continues to live in the world of "self" and "other" needs the dualistic language of "I" and "Thou," even though it does not mirror the deepest truth we know" (Green 2003:15).

Jim believes in God, although not in a "God" who lives in heaven. The divine, for Jim as it is for many skeptical believers, is elusive and metaphorical. In *Teaching Your Children about God: A Modern Jewish Approach*, David Wolpe wrestles with a complicated image of the divine. He writes: "The image of God is precisely that part of the person we cannot point to or name. The spark of the Divine is that which makes you unmistakably you" (Wolpe 1995). Using the word God to name complicated ideas about people and our world seems consistent with a psychoanalytic view of life. But Wolpe also writes "God is the one who made the world" (Wolpe 1995:58).

I don't believe God made the world. Jim seems to sit comfortably with the paradox of feeling God as both an inspirational idea and a personalized deity. I can't. I don't believe in God. Freud writes "religious ideas are teachings and assertions about facts and conditions of external (or internal) reality which tell something one has not discovered from oneself and which lay claim to one's belief" (Freud 1927b:25). In temple, I feel a resistance to prayer, in which I am invited to *believe*, along with everyone around me. In practice it seems that in public prayer, God is invoked as a personal entity. In songs God is watching us from a distance. On inspirational plaques, God carries us through the roughest patches of sand. After baseball games God is thanked for helping out. Again though, I see a similarity between the work of therapists and clergy: although religion may have its head in the sky, it generally has its feet on the ground, concerned with people's lives and the needs of the community. Rabbis sanctify the most important of life's stages: birth, weddings and unions, illness and death.

Just as Judaism has changed with the post-modern era, so has analysis. Although it is unlikely that psychoanalysis was ever generally practiced according to its most austere principles, even by Freud himself, there has been a change in the traditional model. Stephen Mitchell writes: "even though relationality was salient in psychoanalysis from the very beginning, both in theory and in clinical practice, there were long stretches in the history of psychoanalytic ideas in which the nature of human relatedness was not studied and theorized about directly" (Mitchell 2000:ix). As Irwin Hoffman has told us, the book has been thrown away (and perhaps retrieved and dusted off a bit). The baby-watchers have been invited to join the party. The Relationalists are so in that they are being taught here at BPSI in Harry Penn's course called "Object Relations."

A clean division between science and religion doesn't make the same kind of sense in our post-mechanical age world as it did in Freud's time. Even I, a hard-core rationalist, am occasionally open to the wondrous. One of my brothers and one of my sister-in-laws had a fight a few years ago. She was pregnant and espousing the awesome nature of reproduction. He declared that her pregnancy was no more miraculous than a fruit fly's spawning of its offspring. I agreed with both of the warring parties. Although I am most familiar with fruit flies as somewhat disgusting exemplars of Mendelian genetics, the very fact of their existence does seem miraculous. I went to medical school and I am trained as a psychiatrist. I prescribe medications and study neurotransmitters and liver enzyme systems. But sometimes psychopharmacology isn't enough! I want something more. Like Freud, I am jealous of the faithful: "How enviable," he wrote "to those of us who are poor in faith, do those enquirers seem who are convinced of the existence of a Supreme Being!" (Freud 1939[1934-1938]:122). In *A Godless Jew*, Peter Gay writes that Freud could not detect in himself "an indefinable sense of connectedness," an "oceanic feeling of awe before the universe," which he saw as the heart of religious sentiment (Gay 2004:16-17).

Well, I must admit to you all here, that on a good day I feel that sense of connection: with patients, with friends, with my family, and in my own analysis. I come here, to our Temple BPSI; I study our texts diligently; I emulate my teachers and idealize my analyst. The oceanic feeling was strong when I was pregnant and when I finally gave birth to my two sons and got to meet them. I guess it was that

fruit fly feeling—being part of something so utterly
common and yet so divinely amazing and specific. Even if
we don't name it God, I think that many of us believe
something larger than ourselves. A number of our patients
seek treatment not because of their conflicts, but because
of a terrible sense of emptiness. We try to see in our
patients some echo of our own struggles. We work to
recognize and know our analysands and attune ourselves to
reverberate with their thoughts and feelings. Killingmo's
"widening scope of analytic technique" (Killingmo
1989:66) speaks to efforts to help heal patients who suffer
from a deficit in their very sense of self. Perhaps I agree
with Freud's friend and colleague Oskar Pfister, a pastor
and a lay analyst who felt psychoanalysis was a "substitute
religion" (Gay 2004:20). Freud himself allowed that
analysts might be "secular pastoral worker[s]." (Freud
1927a:255).

And yet—there is a difference between a world-view
based on psychoanalysis and on religion. Psychoanalysis
springs from the hermeneutics of suspicion, while religion
has at its core a vision of an ideal: namely God and the
pursuit of a divine standard. Stephen Mitchell writes:
"religious traditions locate meaning in relation to a prime
mover or designer of the universe" (Mitchell 1997:25).
Analysis, at least in theory, values the disruption of ideals
and standards, without a reference to a particular ethical
model. Like Goldilocks I have found in psychoanalysis
something that seems just right, while religion feels too
hot, and portfolio management too cold.

A couple of weeks ago, after I had had a personal loss,
I dreamt that I was walking along a frozen Vermont field
in the middle of the night. I was not frightened. I heard a
crackling and looked back to find that my husband Jim was
coming, keeping pace a hundred yards behind me. He then
caught up with me and we walked across a dirt road to a
gathering of friends. They were cooking around an orange
fire, which glowed against the grey sky and ground. When
I awoke, I had the sense that this dream was a visitation or

a gift. In the liminal space of my sleep I could access a spiritual part of myself. And in the light of day I still enjoy playing the role of the rational, and yes, atheist physician, in the best spirit of our sainted Sigmund Freud.

References

Freud, S. (1927a) The Question of Lay Analysis – Postscript. *Standard Edition*, Volume 20.

Freud, S. (1927b) The Future of an Illusion. *Standard Edition*, Volume 21.

Freud, S. (1933 [1932]) New Introductory Lectures on Psycho-Analysis: Lecture 35, The Question of a *Weltanschauung. Standard Edition*, Volume 22.

Freud, S. (1939[1934-1938]) Moses and Monotheism. *Standard Edition* Volume 23.

Gay, P. (2004) *A Godless Jew: Freud, Atheism, and the Making of Psychoanalysis.* New Haven: Yale University Press.

Green, A. (2003) *Seek My Face: A Jewish Mystical Theology.* Woodstock, VT: Jewish Lights Publishing.

Killingmo, B. (1989) Conflict and Deficit: Implications for Technique. *Int. J. Psychoanal.* 70:65-79.

Mitchell, S. (1997) *Influence and Autonomy in Psychoanalysis.* Hillsdale, NJ: Analytic Press.

Mitchell, S. (2000). *Relationality: From Attachment to Intersubjectivity.* Hillsdale, NJ: Analytic Press.

Wolpe, David. (1995) *Teaching Your Children about God: A Modern Jewish Approach.* New York: Harper.

CRIS RATINER

I recently tuned in one of the satellite movie channels to catch about three minutes worth of *The Seven Percent Solution*, and was completely tickled to see Alan Arkin playing Freud. Alan Arkin is cute, and has always conveyed a sense of warm cuddliness. I found myself embracing the picture of Freud as a cute, wry, thoughtful philosopher and humanitarian. Yes! That must be him. What a nice person he must have been. Oh he's not so intimidating after all. Wow, after all these years of reading to discover that Freud was someone I could imagine having at a dinner party. But *wait*!!!! Alan Arkin *isn't* Freud!!!

However sincere a performance that was, it did not capture the intellectual intensity, sadness, occasional irascibility and entertaining combination of pride and humility that I hear in Freud's work. Arkin's Freud was undoubtedly his representation of the Freud *he* imagined.

Now, I'll embarrass myself, but there's a *Star Trek* episode in which Freud plays a significant role—he appears as himself, in a hologram, in order to help Data the android interpret his dreams. When I watched this episode, I was initially thrilled to hear the revered name. I sat rapt in front of the television, excitedly thinking that one of my serious pleasures and my frivolous pleasures could be melded together. By the end of the episode I was let down, hearing yet again about the famous cigar that is just a cigar, and watching Freud depicted yet again as just a cranky philosopher and ineffective old relic.

Both of these incidents caught me off guard. And then recalled me to Freud—the "real" Freud—the one I've encountered time and time again, who resists all efforts to be caricatured, trivialized, or even simplified. This has been my most repetitive and enduring experience reading Freud: finding a voice so original, so human, so deep and authentic that attempts to "sum him up" or "cut him down to size" or "poke fun at him" inevitably fall flat.

This discovery began long before coming to BPSI. As a confused and unhappy 12-year-old budding psychologist, I went to the local library to read about "the brain," and found references to someone who used the Latin words "ego" and "id" like they meant something real—more than an upcoming vocabulary quiz. As a 20-something trying to decide between medical school, graduate school and law school, I scoured the psych library and discovered that the psychiatric journals seemed narrow and ruled by nosology, while the academic psychology journals specialized in the "yeah, duh" variety of research. Feeling a bit like Goldilocks, I found the psychoanalytic journals "just right". They had the tone, the depth, the theoretical strength and compassion I sought. So, I figured all would be clear if I just read Freud himself.

I was confused. He wasn't easy, and didn't explain everything. There was no panacea, no explanation of my own distress and no clearly delineated path to happiness. He didn't make it clear how I could translate what I read into a job, or whether I'd be any good at helping anybody. Nonetheless, I did get the idea that he was at the heart of so much I found valuable, and tucked his presence away in my head.

A famous undergraduate professor of developmental psychology seemed to promise understanding. We read "An Outline of Psycho-Analysis" (Freud 1940[1938]) for class. But he confused me even more, his synopsis of Freud being that Americans have always misread Freud, and that he represented, in fact, deterministic bad news, in contrast to the behaviorists, who supposedly offered the "good news" that anything could be changed, learned or rectified. I felt lost, and in over my head. The only sensible option I could think of was to throw myself in further, so I applied to the most psychoanalytically inclined doctoral program I could find.

I had the very good fortune in my first semester to be taught by someone many of you know—Murray Cohen—who presented, explicated and elucidated Freud's works, sometimes in mesmerizing fashion. He knew so much and could keep it all straight! At the beginning I even wondered if, in fact, Murray wasn't actually Freud himself. I figured that was pretty cool—it was almost like going back in time to catch sight of the genius. Just as when I watched Alan Arkin, I wanted to make Freud easier and more accessible by seeing Murray as his avatar. Of course, it didn't work. I sat in class pondering this. But, as I began to read more, wrote my papers, and began my clinical work, Murray's voice and Freud's voice diverged (especially around my dissertation). Murray's voice became the mentor, scholar and clinical supervisor I knew in 'real' time, and Freud's voice became the scientist, theoretician and thinker of his time—a voice from another era whose genius travels well.

None of the representations of Freud ever stand up to the original.

I think of all the annoying cartoons I've seen over the years—the vast majority of which had something to do with the cigar line. They'd drive me nuts, and I'd always want to go on the defensive, proving to philistines that he really was a genius. I'd always bristled at the way they trivialized and caricatured a thinker who'd had such a huge impact on my life.

Even academics who work from Freud in their scholarship, and who keep Freud alive through their hermeneutics present a different Freud than the one I know. For instance, a book reviewer (Weber 1996) writing about essays on Restoration comedy said:

> Freud plays a particularly important role in Gill's analysis of the issues raised by interpreting ladies on the Restoration stage. Using his discussion of jokes, Gill maintains that satiric comedy fuses Freud's two

varieties of the tendentious joke, the hostile and the obscene, creating a verbal seduction in which male aggression triumphs over female weakness. According to Gill, women can never perpetrate these jokes—indeed, "the woman becomes the necessarily excluded object of the joke" (Weber and Gill 1994)—but can only be their victims, for the conclusion of manners comedy invariably depends on the public exposure of private female sexual activity. Women become the butt of the satiric joke that structures the comic plot, their vulnerability and passivity reinstating the masculine integrity, privilege, and subjectivity that have been questioned in the course of the play.

It's a relief to find someone who takes Freud seriously, but while cogent and well-informed, I read a paragraph like this and my brain shuts down. How *does* so much get lost in translation? And these aren't even the "Freud-bashers" of the world, who, generally without aid of having actually read any of Freud's works, deride, ridicule and demonize his contribution, banishing him from the imaginary Eden of empiricism and evidence-based treatment.

I probably didn't need to get so worked up over all this. What I've learned, above all, is that Freud speaks for himself, with authenticity, intelligence and integrity.

Not that many years ago I went to the Anna Freud house in Hempstead for the first time. It was a disconcerting experience: Freud the writer, scientist and teacher lived in multiple guises in my brain. Coming in contact with his actual possessions, books and oriental covered couch left me wondrous and disoriented. How could that actually be the *actual* couch? The *real* office? I half feared and expected to have a religious experience: I was poised to feel enlightened and awed; my oppositional self longed to be cynically unimpressed. Instead, I felt neither. I found myself reacting as myself: I loved the height of the ceiling, the richness of the carpets, the heft of the library. The historical artifacts were dizzying. And, as I looked at all the statues and remnants of history, I felt sad, and a little sobered. Freud couldn't have been more aware of the barbarity of humankind, and yet he managed to prevent it from contaminating his theorizing. His *sadness* comes through in the writings, and he cannot be shrugged off as a dry, abstruse philosopher.

That warmth and compassion never gets captured by the popular jokes. Nor, for that matter does the depth of his thinking. Or his wit. Or humor.

This last year has only intensified and repeated my experience on a weekly basis. I've looked at our syllabus on a Wednesday night, and find myself bleary thinking about all the reading. I lull myself into thinking I can skim the piece, take away a few major points, and 'get it.' As usual, this doesn't work, and I find, time after time, that the power of Freud's ideas virtually hits me on the head.

Sometimes when I'm engaged in serious procrastination and work avoidance, I'll pick a volume of Freud off the shelf and open it randomly. It never fails to amaze me how quickly that voice appears. The first few sentences I read will seem dense and dry, then with the second few I'll cotton to what he's saying. Next, I'll feel overwhelmed by the richness of the ideas, and a bit baffled as well. And, just when I'm ready to put the book down and return to the task at hand, the sincerity and clarity of Freud will knock me over. There's always something that reaches out from the page to rivet me—and I discover that voice anew.

References

Freud, S. (1940[1938])   An Outline of Psycho-Analysis. *Standard Edition*, Volume 22.

Weber, H. (1996).   [Review of *Interpreting Ladies: Women, Wit, and Morality in the Restoration Comedy of Manners*, by Patricia Gill (1994)]. *Criticism*, Winter.

LAURA CRAIN

When my friends learned that I was studying to become a psychoanalyst, they came bearing gifts. I received a number of Freud finger puppets, as well as a Jung puppet and a Couch puppet—apparently so that Freud and Jung could take turns analyzing each other. I received a tin box of "After Therapy Mints" featuring a picture of Freud relaxing on his couch, enjoying a mint—maybe after a particularly satisfying hour with some lucky imagined person. I also received from a nine-year friend of my older son a very durable plastic Freud action figure. This was a five-inch replica of Freud with movable arms, a long gray coat, and holding a cigar, of course. Significantly, I had seen that very same action figure on my analyst's bookshelf, and I was aware of being pleased to now have my very own. As these gifts began to occupy space on my coffee table, I thought about how the news of my spending time with Freud had impacted my friends.

Spending time with Freud also began to impact my husband and children as I began to abandon them on Thursday nights to a place where, I explained to my children, I would learn how to help people talk about their troubles. My older son followed along with interest my E-Bay purchase of Freud's *Standard Edition*; he was intrigued that no one had bid against me. He felt that I must've gotten a "good deal," but he wondered why there hadn't been more competition for the prize. Later, he asked me who this man Freud was, this prolific writer who was responsible for that tall stack of blue books that arrived in the mail. I replied to him something like, "Freud was a very brilliant man who lived a long time ago, and understood all about how the mind worked." He replied "Well, how could he know how my mind works if he's dead?" I re-

plied that this was an amazing thing and that Freud was a
scientist of the mind. I said that Science meant something
that you could use to explain things over and over again. I
don't know how deeply I felt that at the time since psychoanalysis can seem more like an art than a science to me,
but I was aware that I wanted my son to feel that Freud
was the great psychoanalytic scientist.

One Thursday evening I returned to a quiet house—
everyone was asleep. In the quietness, I came upon a remarkable scene. I found that my plastic Freud action figure had been spirited away from its spot on the coffee table and was hanging by one foot from a string attached to
a plastic fire truck in my sons' bathtub. Apparently, Freud
saw a lot of action that evening. The tub was littered with
other figures, much smaller LEGO or Playmobil type figures surrounding the drying Freud in his inauspicious position.

Oddly, I felt compelled to free Freud and put him back
on the coffee table—after all, this was MY toy. I found
my mind full of fantasies of what the play had meant. Was
my son expressing his aggression towards Freud, who had
in his fantasy taken me away from him that evening because he knew that I was away learning about Freud? How
would my analyst react if I told him the story? Would he
insist that I actually wanted to hang him by his foot from a
fire truck and I was actually talking about having aggressive feelings towards him? I admit to some pleasure imag-
ining this sadistic image, and tried to shake it from my
mind. Why was I forgetting that it had been my son, not
me, that had been playing in the tub that evening? Even
worse, since I already knew that I did have aggressive feelings towards my analyst, did my son know too? How
could he know? Could I actually undo those aggressive
feelings that I had toward my analyst and toward my son,
who had stolen MY action figure, by freeing the Freud action figure? I began to realize that my associations about
what had been done with the Freud action figure could be
understood using Freudian theory. Freud suddenly seemed

to be in the air, in the fabric of my life, and that felt like a new way of seeing Freud, for me.

My relationship with Freud had a very rocky start having been taught as a child that Freud was subversive to the religious teachings that I heard on Sunday mornings. The one psychiatrist in our neighborhood was known to my family only as the guy who had sold us a used car that broke down less than one year later. That same psychiatrist had always displayed a larger than life Santa in a gigantic sleigh on his front porch every December. Was that his reaction formation talisman against the watered down anti-Semitism in my community? Or was it his protection against the feelings he knew that people in my neighborhood had about Freud? From this neighborhood, my journey toward psychoanalysis was circuitous, but inexorable.

At the beginning of my psychiatric training, Freud seemed forbidden, subversive, intriguing, dense, and indecipherable. I particularly remember my first real intellectual exposure to Freud in a class called "Models of the Mind" in my first year of residency training. What stands out for me is a sleep deprived moment sitting in what is now called the Hackett Room at Massachusetts General Hospital, listening, post call, in a dream-like state to a psychiatrist wearing a massive white coat. He was drawing pictures on a chalkboard of Freud's model of the mind featuring blob-like images of the preconscious and the conscious. At that moment, 15 years ago, Freud seemed so very far away—his picture of the mind, like blobs of different colored Play Doh, seemed at the time to have nothing to do with me or any patients I had ever seen—an unwelcome intrusion at a time when I simply needed to sleep. I had been up all of the night before containing agitated mentally ill patients in the emergency room with shots of Haldol and Ativan, locked rooms, and restraints. So much action, no reflection, in that emergency room; no time to understand what had brought these individuals into their action-oriented states. How could I use Freud's theories then to understand or help? But thinking about all of this now, it was all there—Freud's ideas were there in my mind, but in a state that would be hard to untangle by a bleary eyed psychiatrist in training.   In stark contrast, I think of Cordelia Schmidt-Hellerau drawing diagrams on the chalkboard in a recent Freud class here at BPSI to illustrate Freud's model of the mind. I think of Freud classes with Rita Teusch, Jim Dalsimer, Steve Sternbach, and Mark Goldblatt. In those classes, I felt awake, alive, full of new understanding, finding pleasure in discussion with my classmates and knowing how very relevant Freud's ideas are in my daily work with patients.   I think about how far my relationship with Freud has come.

Similarly, at that moment Thursday evening, in my living room, picking up my plastic Freud from the scene of the bathtub crime, he seemed to be alive in my relationship with my sons. My sons who knew nothing of Freud and were unknown to him, yet could demonstrate to me the very things that Freud understood about them. I decided that I should return the action figure to the tub, but leave it standing in the soap holder in a more dignified vertical position. I felt certain that a child analyst would have insisted that I leave Freud hanging where he was, but my guilt about all of my own aggression was too great. The next day, I of course had to inquire of my children what the play had been about. I learned that this had been a joint venture between both of my sons—ages 6 and 9 at the time. I can't remember all of the details of it but it went something like this: there had been a terrible fire in the bathtub that evening that had put all of the smaller action figures in grave danger. Freud had arrived in the fire truck to save everyone. There was an awful lot of water—splashing, flooding of the bathroom which had brought my husband in to settle things down and spoil some of the fun. In the play, even though things seemed to be going pretty well, a bad guy arrived. Freud, from his position on the cherry picker of the Fisher-Price truck, despite all of the good he had done, was shot by the bad guy. He fell, and even though he was still alive, he was left hanging by one foot from a machine, as a supervisor of mine pointed out, designed to pull the cherries off of trees—all in an ordinary night of play.

Was the bad guy me, who had left my children, or an immediate reaction to my husband who had put a stop to the wild splashing? Who did Freud represent in my sons' minds? Obviously, there had been a conflict about whether or not to kill him that was left unresolved. Was Freud coming between me and my sons since I had been here at BPSI, away from them? Was their conscious objective to be rid of Freud, or was Freud a stand in for my husband, who also stood between me and my sons, and my son's actual unconscious objective was to get rid of my husband, sublimated by their play with Freud? Were my sons counting on me to rescue Freud and did they experience relief that I had cut him down? There was no protest about my doing this despite my fantasy of what a child analyst would say. Even more, could all of these things be true at the same time? When I told my analyst the story, I had the wish that he would be entertained. He did not gratify my wishes with an expression of laughter. He offered me much more than that. He allowed me the freedom of my own thoughts and feelings to find meaning in the story that I had brought to him. It was his job to be my psychoanalyst.

I became more and more impressed by how much meaning could be made of all of this, and Freud seemed to be at the center. How ironic that it would be me rescuing the Freud action figure, when I had grown up with so much hostility within my family and community about what Freud understood about the mind? How ironic that all of this thinking and feeling was centered around the action figure and that, in fact, there was really no action being taken at all, rather thoughts and feelings were arising from within my own mind. In a way more courageous and brilliant than anyone ever has, Freud encouraged us all to realize the riches in store for us when we restrain our actions and stretch ourselves to understand our own thoughts and feelings, as well as our patients' thoughts and feelings. Even more, he understood what we could gain when we restrain our actions as we conduct ourselves in civilization.

I am not facile regarding theoretical ideas. It is as if clinical experience and life experience has to collide with the theory over and over again to impact me and become real for me. What a valuable gift it is to be able to see Freud's relevance in the world. Sometimes, it is as if we have our own private Freud in our theoretical minds and we are reluctant to share him—just as I felt reluctant to share my action figure with my children. I feel that I have collided with Freud over and over in my life and in my training. Indeed, we all collide with Freud's amazing insights every day about who we are and what we may be capable of becoming.

ANTON KRIS

It is a great pleasure to welcome all of you to this com-memoration of Freud's 150th birthday. When Pat Wright and Jack Beinashowitz invited me to participate in this event, we soon agreed to create a faculty version of the candidates' "Academic Lecture" of last June, "Freud and Me." We will begin with a very brief video clip of Freud, at his 82nd birthday, May 6th 1938, a few weeks before he left Vienna for London, where he died the following year on September 23rd, 1939. This clip will be followed by a video clip of the 100th birthday celebration at 20 Mares-field Gardens, his London home, May 6, 1956. Watch for Ernest Jones pulling the flag to reveal the medallion newly affixed to the front of the house that proclaims it as Freud's last residence. You will be interested, too, in a moment that shows three women analysts speaking cor-dially at a table in the garden: Marie Bonaparte, Anna Freud, and Melanie Klein. The amateur photographer was my mother, Marianne Kris, and you will recognize a good deal about her personality in the frequency with which her lens focused on the many children present along with the important grownups.

Before I call on the three panelists to give us their views, I would like briefly to say a word about my own. Freud was a very close friend of my maternal grandfather, Oskar Rie, a slightly younger colleague, with whom Freud wrote a book on the cerebral diplegias of childhood and who became the pediatrician of his children. Until Oskar's death in 1931, Freud inscribed and sent him each of his reprints.

Freud was also the friend and teacher of my parents, whose contributions to psychoanalysis are known to most of you. Through them and through other students and

35

through his writings, he exerted the most important influence on my own work, as well.

Freud's writings and the psychoanalytic method he invented became a giant influence on the whole 20th century world. As W. H. Auden (1940) put it in his memorial: "to us he is no more a person/now but a whole climate of opinion."

I will not recite to you his achievements that you know so well, starting with the use of free association for investigation and the demonstration of unconscious mental life, especially unconscious conflict, and the phenomena of transference and resistance. Nor shall I speak of the many changes that have separated us from him in the 67 years since his death. Here I want to express my awe for the *way* he worked and formulated his findings, casting such a very wide net, overcoming internal resistance, holding to truthfulness, maintaining an open system, tolerating uncertainty, recognizing the importance of development, the body, and metaphor. He remains an extraordinary model for new work and new theoretical formulation in our field.

References

Auden, W. H. (1940) *Another Time*. London: Faber and Faber.

CORDELIA SCHMIDT-HELLERAU

I will never forget the day I "met" Freud. I was seventeen. It was a beautiful summer afternoon, and I had taken a long walk with a friend, discussing all the big questions that worked on our minds: life, love and death, truth, justice, politics and perhaps some more. When we finally returned to my home my friend reached into his jacket and pulled out a slim pocket book. "I have something for you," he said, "I'm sure you'll like it." It was "An Outline of Psycho-Analysis" (Freud 1940[1938]). I was immediately interested. It was 1968, the times of the students' revolution in Europe. The newspapers and magazines were full of big names like Marx and Hegel, Marcuse and Adorno, Sartre and Freud, and I hadn't studied any of these giants. I thought this Outline would provide me with a neat summary of Freud's thoughts that I was eager to learn about. And so, as if the challenges of our afternoon conversation hadn't been enough, I immediately started to read. Well reading isn't the right word—I rather struggled, studied or worked hard to get through the first pages. The "Outline" is not an easy start into Freud's work at age seventeen. But eventually I got through it, and as little as I understood of it at the time, Freud's way of thinking, his mind completely fascinated me. I wanted to learn more about his psychoanalysis. And I think it was with this first book that I decided: I want to become a psychoanalyst.

From these early days on, I never stopped reading Freud. I did so during my studies of literature and philosophy and even more so when I studied psychology; I immersed myself still deeper into his work during my analytic training, and now I continue to do so when I am writing and teaching. And even though I have read many of his essays many times, I never feel bored by them. In fact, it happens more often than not that I discover something new in a text I am most familiar with: a short side remark that sketches an intriguing idea, I hadn't noticed before; a contradiction of sorts that makes me wonder; a connection that suddenly opens a window to a new perspective; a remark that makes me smile, sometimes even laugh out aloud. Freud has such a wonderful, wise and dry humor. Time and again I am touched by his wisdom, his empathy with human weakness, his sympathy for the child's struggle to understand the world, and his appreciation for the mind's creativity—be it in its most pathological or perverse expressions. An author is said to be a classic when his or her work is inexhaustible. No doubt, Freud is one of the great classics of the twentieth century.

Freud and Me—the title of this birthday celebration asks for a personal take on him or his work. So why was it Freud (and not, for example, Jung, Adler, Fromm or anybody else) who captivated my mind? As a child I always wanted to know how things work, how they come about? I wanted to understand why people—certainly first of all my parents—were how they were and did what they did. There are many possible questions on a child's mind: who-questions (like "who plays with me?"), what-questions (like "what to do now?"), where-questions (like "where to go from here?"). I was one of those kids who tirelessly asked these why-questions: why are things as they are? Much later I learned from Freud's beautiful essay "On the Sexual Theories of Children" (Freud 1908)—still one of my favorites—what all these questions on a deeper level were about. Yet even then and throughout my life, these why-questions are the ones that intrigue me most—and I actually gave one of my articles this title "Why aggression?" (Schmidt-Hellerau 2002). When I first read Freud and ever since I found him asking these kinds of questions, passionately searching for the ways and reasons for all the small and not so small riddles posed to us by the human mind. Why does someone continuously forget the name of a particular person? How does an odd slip with a crude sexual innuendo come about in a serious official conversation? Why do we dream at all, and why about long forgotten childhood events, and why in these strange scenarios? How can we understand that one patient is afraid of a danger that objectively doesn't seem to exist, or that another suffers from a relationship she nevertheless clings to for decades, or that still another can't stop obsessing about something and cripples his whole life because of it? Why is that so, why do they do this?

Freud was tackling all these questions, patiently and persistently. And he did this by almost freely associating in writing. In fact I would think of his prose as "free scientific association": Free association here means that in his work he didn't shy away from making use of all sorts of sources: first and foremost, of course, his clinical experiences; but he also related to religion, mythology, literature, art, history, evolution, biology, neurophysiology and everyday life experiences. To use and revert the current economical term of "out-sourcing", we could say: drawing from a broad variety of different fields, all created by the human mind, Freud was "in-sourcing" a wide range of psychological wisdom in his relentless effort to trace and map the workings of the mind.

As you all know, free association, first formulated 1895 in "Studies on Hysteria" (Freud 1895), revolutionized the treatment of neuroses—Tony Kris (1996[1982]) wrote a wonderful book on it, a must on every analyst's reading list. And in the same year 1895 Freud theoretically elaborated the mechanisms of associations in "A Project for a Scientific Psychology" (1950[1895]), thereby minutely describing the processes of all mental (and neuronal) activity. Freud understood that associations, as free as possible, can reveal the secrets of the mind—in its unconscious content as well as in its working principles.

Consequently Freud made use of the method of free association as his most appropriate research tool in "The Interpretation of Dreams" (1900). But also later he continued to use free association in his theoretical and clinical papers: Whatever came to his mind, it seems, while he was working on a particular problem, the very fact that it did, indicated to him that there could be some common kernel: the associated idea could be a stepping stone to the resolution of the problem at stake. And so Freud picks it up and includes it in his thinking. Thus, his work is not only about how the mind works but simultaneously documents the working of the mind.

This way of doing science was and is different from what science had ever done before—and many have criticized him for being unscientific. But this method is scientific. Freud makes use of his associations in a controlled way. When he uses analogy, he is always aware that this is merely analogy, sometimes he even calls it a weak argument. He specifies in which way an association may further his exploration of a problem. He allows himself to be guided by it for a while, but he easily drops it if it doesn't prove to be valuable for his task. His writing is scientific because he always remains focused on building his argument and following the laws of logic (even though he fails in this at times). Logic and consistency are, like mathematics, the decisive tools of all scientific work. Finally Freud's work is scientific in its goal to reveal, capture and describe the general laws of mental functioning.

Now Freud, associating scientifically in writing, allowed me, the reader, to think with him his thoughts, to follow his pros and cons, to try an idea and to reject it a few pages later. Thus reading these texts itself becomes an exercise in associating —which includes our freedom to stop at any point and to think: Wait a minute, is this really convincing? Why did he drop this previous assumption now? Or does this fit to what the clinical material shows etc.? Freud asks these questions, and we can ask them too and then rejoin him in continuing to read. Thus reading Freud is continuously stimulating. Freud's work is not a monument. It is a living and growing organism; it has produced a huge amount of literature (not only within psychoanalysis) that has deepened and broadened our insight into psychic life. And if you ever feel like writing an essay, and you don't really know what you want to write about, just pick up, I would say, any essay of Freud. Read it carefully, and make Freud work, as the French would say, that is, let your mind work while reading, and within a short time you will have an intriguing subject for your paper. In fact I feel Freud's stimulating work is created by one of the freest minds I've ever met. It is in particular his freedom of thinking that I love; I can say he was my most important teacher. His thinking informed my mind and opened it for the freedom to do further work with his work and on my own.

With his specific way of thinking, moving dialectically between clinical experience and theoretical conceptualization, Freud outlined what I would see as the most comprehensive, differentiated and sophisticated model of how the mind works as a whole, from its micro-level, for instance in his "Project" (1950 [1895]), to its macro-level, for instance in "The Ego and the Id" (1923). Within this model he elaborates the filigree of healthy and pathological psychic processes, based on the two axiomatic assumptions of drives and structures. The drives stand for the energetic and dynamic aspect of the mind, its connection with the body—all that creates movement of any kind, the movements of our thoughts as well as the movements of us toward our objects. The structures stand for the relative stability of our psyche; they form and contain our thoughts, fantasies, feelings and actions, our memories, our representations of self and object.

It goes without saying that Freud didn't always get it right. Who would? My response to the contradictions, logical breaks and consistency cracks in Freud's work has been to ask "why?" To ask this question meant to work through his metapsychological writings trying to resolve some of the problems he left us with. I did this in an adventure that lasted more than seven years and got me most intensely involved in an ongoing dialogue with Freud's thinking. It was one of the most exciting challenges I had ever taken on, and resulted in a book (Schmidt-Hellerau, 2001) that theory freaks more than others enjoy reading. As many of you might know, from this work but also very much from my work with my patients, a special focus of my interest has emerged. It is drive theory, and in particular the exploration of the preservative drives, a crucial concept, it seems to me, that Freud first neglected and then, after 1920, sort of forgot by merging it with sexuality under the umbrella of Eros, the life drives. I think because of this theoretical move (Freud, 1920) we've got a blind spot in our clinical perception. Our clinical perception is hampered if we lack a concept to capture it. What if we didn't have the concept of infantile sexuality or the Oedipus complex? Would we see and understand what goes on right in front of our eyes? That's why I believe if we want to be psychoanalysts, we cannot choose to be just clinicians. We have to grapple with theory, with our understanding of the mind's working, for instance with the question: what drives our patients? I think if we include self- and object-preservation as powerful drive activities in our theoretical and clinical thinking, a new window will open. There will be much to discover, much work to be done, much more than one person alone could possibly handle.

Finally, can we, still today, relate to Freud's work, a work that goes a century back, without being hopelessly outdated? Can we appreciate his work and get stimulated by it and still be critical and find our own way of thinking? My answer is yes. Like a good father he gave us enough to get us going and to work our ways as psychoanalysts. I am grateful for this inheritance. Happy Birthday, dear old Freud!

References

Freud, S. (1895). Studies on Hysteria. *Standard Edition*, Volume 3.

Freud, S. (1900). The Interpretation of Dreams. *Standard Edition*, Volumes 4-5.

Freud, S. (1908). On the Sexual Theories of Children. *Standard Edition*, Volume 9.

Freud, S. (1920). Beyond the Pleasure Principle. *Standard Edition*, Volume 18.

Freud, S. (1923). The Ego and the Id. *Standard Edition*, Volume 19.

Freud, S. (1940) An Outline of Psycho-Analysis. *Standard Edition*, Volume 23.

Freud, S. (1950 [1895]). A Project of a Scientific Psychology. *Standard Edition*, Volume 1.

Kris, A. (1996 [1982]) *Free Association. Method and Process*. Revised and expanded edition. London: Karnac Books.

Schmidt-Hellerau, C. (2001) *Life Drive & Death Drive, Libido & Lethe*. A formalized consistent model of psychoanalytic drive and structure theory. New York: Other Press.

Schmidt-Hellerau, C. (2002) Why Aggression? *Int. J. of Psychoanal.* 83:1269-89.

ANNA ORNSTEIN

In order for me to speak about Freud's influence on my current theoretical orientation and clinical work, I have to tell you about the Institute I attended and its theoretical orientation at that time.

I am a graduate of the Chicago Institute for Psychoanalysis where I finished five years of course work and the required number of supervisory hours in 1969. However, I did not graduate until 1971 because the Chicago Institute had rather stringent requirements for graduation. We had to take an examination in which, sitting in a class room, we were handed out about 6 (what I remember as rather tough) questions. I took a year to prepare for this exam during which time I reviewed most of Freud and what at that time was a very extensive literature on ego psychology. I graduated in 1971 after finishing a paper which was another graduation requirement. I shall come back to the theme of this paper because it best represents Freud's influence on my thinking as well as the transition I experienced in the early 70s from a very traditional, classical psychoanalytic theory to self psychology.

I had four patients in supervised analyses and I am proud of the fact that all four came to termination. My supervisors were superb clinicians and teachers. Kohut was not among them. I was supervised by Kohut after I finished my training. During my training, I took a Freud course with Kohut in my second year. His Freud course was the most popular course at the Institute. His teaching method was old fashioned European: he could not be interrupted and we had to ask questions only two weeks later when we had a chance to study the material he covered. No idle speculations here but a very serious study of the text. Kohut's knowledge and understanding of Freud was considered to be the best at the Institute. And, as you may know, Kohut was also a committed ego psychologist who could make that theory come clinically alive. He always had a strong clinical focus. If Freud was our Bible—and it was—then ego psychology, especially the works of Hartmann, Kris and Loewenstein, were our sacred commentaries.

It was in relation to the clinical ramifications of ego psychology: the importance of the level of ego organization, an appreciation for the centrality of transference in clinical work, and mainly, it was in relation to ego psychology's emphasis on the analysis of defense that I had made the transition from traditional to psychoanalytic self psychology.

I was not familiar with Paul Gray's work at that time but I followed the research by Sampson and Weisz and was a discussant at one of their control-mastery conferences in San Francisco.

Our Institute was careful in distinguishing between Oedipal (high level ego organization) and pre-Oedipal psychopathology. And in keeping with the times, only psychopathology that had its roots in the faulty resolution of the Oedipus complex was considered to be analyzable. After taking extensive histories, we filled out pages and pages of questionnaires regarding analyzability. If you think about the importance we give today to the transference (specifically, what becomes activated in a particular analytic dyad), you have to wonder how a decision regarding analyzability could have been (or should have been) made on the basis of history.

It was instructive for me to re-read the case summaries we had to prepare after the first six months of the analysis and then a final one at the time of termination. These summaries had to demonstrate the presence of a Transference Neurosis that was supposed to have replicated the original Infantile Neurosis. Only when we could demonstrate that the transference in the analysis arose in relation to the unconscious fantasies associated with the Oedipus complex, did we get credit for the analysis of the patient.

A good example for this was my second control, a 33 year old man who presented with partial impotence and premature ejaculation. Because of the sexual nature of his presenting problem, my supervisor expected him to develop sexual fantasies about me. This would have been evidence that the Transference Neurosis was indeed a repetition of the Infantile Neuroses, that repressed sexual fantasies related to the mother were reactivated in relation to me, a female analyst, and could now, in the analysis, be resolved by interpretations.

I believe that if our education would not have focused so narrowly on Freud and Ego Psychology, we may not have greeted Kohut's ideas with the same enthusiasm as we did. We knew practically nothing about the British Object Relations theories other than Winnicott's. Melanie Klein's ideas were ridiculed because of her early timing of the Oedipus complex and the heavy emphasis on infantile aggression. We learned from Michael Balint only because he was Visiting Professor at the Department of Psychiatry in Cincinnati where Paul and I worked. Balint and his books on pre-oedipal issues prepared us for Kohut. Balint and the other object relationists helped us appreciate the significance of pre-oedipal pathology at the time when fewer and fewer patients presented with symptoms that could be traced to problems related to the oedipal phase of development.

Beautiful and convincing as the descriptions of the pre-oedipal pathology were in the literature from the British Schools, they did not offer a clinical handle on these problems as they did not offer the specific transferences that could be expected to arise in relation to them. Pre-oedipal transferences continued to be considered to be regressions from the Oedipal, and since they were considered non-verbal they required parameters, that is, preparatory psychotherapy before analysis.

It was in this analytic atmosphere that Kohut articulated the nature of the selfobject transferences which, at first, he called "narcissistic transferences." Patients who did not fit into the classical conceptualization of psychoneurosis, he said, also developed transferences but of a different kind. His recognition of these (narcissistic) transferences led Kohut—as it led Freud in relation to Dora— to consider the transference as the analyst's primary data; data that when understood in its origin and explicated, constituted the basis for the articulation of a psychoanalytic theory.

In our minds, the selfobject concept changed all aspects of traditional psychoanalytic theory. Most importantly, rather than considering the drives as initiating and propelling psychological development, in this theory, the human infant was assumed to be hard-wired to elicit developmentally needed environmental responses in order to develop a well structured, cohesive self that is optimally functional in the particular society and culture in which it will live. Conceptually, the environment moved into the inner world and structuralization was understood to unfold in the reciprocal interaction between the infant's constitutional givens and an empathically responsive environment.

Selfobject transferences are the expressions of the insufficiently or faultily structuralized mind; they represent expectations that in the analytic situation developmentally needed experiences will provide compensatory psychological structures. This focus on the structure of the self (its cohesion, vigor and aliveness) expanded the spectrum of conditions that analysts could treat analytically without the parameters.

I shall now return to the topic of my graduation paper. Here, timing was of essence. In 1971, just as I was working on my paper, Kohut's first book *The Analysis of the Self* was published. The book contains the detailed descriptions of the various selfobject transferences but it does not have anything about defense and resistance. For Kohut, the answer was obvious: every analyst knows about defense and resistance; he did not think that his first book needed to include this topic. I, however, did not think the matter was so simple. After all, we now thought of the function of defenses very differently from traditional psychoanalysis. In traditional theory, defenses are viewed as mental mechanisms that had become established to hide (repress, deny, project) an unacceptable impulse related to drive-created unconscious fantasies. In self psychology, on the other hand, defenses are viewed as protecting a vulnerable self from fragmentation. The wording and phrasing of interpretations would have to be different from these two different perspectives. For me, the question was this: How do we respond interpretively to mental mechanisms and symptoms that protect the self from fragmentation but, at the same time, they constitute the greatest obstacles to change?

With the help of a clinical example, in a paper titled "The Dread to Repeat and the New Beginning" (1974, revised in 1991), I described how I conceptualized the inclusion of defenses in the interpretive process when the case is conceptualized from a self psychological perspective where the maintenance of empathy-based formulations of interpretations is of primary importance.

In subsequent publications, some jointly with Paul and some individually, I examined the manner in which the interpretive process has to be responsive to our changed view of development and psychopathology; the change in theory called for a change in the conceptualization of the analytic process. Theory, in our view, in addition to the analyst's personality, affects all aspects of practice: the ambience that is created and the wording and phrasing of interpretations. Once we consider that defenses protect a vulnerable self rather than hide unacceptable impulses, interpretive comments would have to be made fairly consistently from within the patient's perspective rather than from the perspective of the external observer.

I am convinced that without my appreciation of Freud's original ideas regarding repression, the ongoing influence of the dynamic unconscious on symptom and character formation, and ego psychology's emphasis on defense and resistance, I would not have focused on these particular issues throughout my professional life. The interpretive process related to defense organizations, and with this, the process of working through and therapeutic action, remains my major preoccupation until this day.

When I reflect on the great gift that we have been given by Freud with his initial and ever evolving theories of the mind and the method he handed to us when he outlined the features of psychoanalytic technique, I believe we have been given one of the remarkable gifts of the 20th Century. We have been extraordinarily fortunate to see in our lifetime how this theory and technique blossomed and how it had become ever more effective in helping our patients. It will be up to future generations not only to preserve this legacy but to recognize its potentials for change.

References

Kohut, H. (1971)   *The Analysis of the Self.: A Systematic Approach to the Psychoanalytic Treatment of Narcissistic Personality Disorders.* New York: IUP.

Ornstein. A. (1974).   The Dread to Repeat and the New Beginning. *Annual of Psychoanalysis* 2:231-248.

STEPHEN STERNBACH

The name Freud designates a person—a heroic investigator—and a groundbreaking body of work. In both of these ways, Freud has been in my life, for many years, an inspiration and an important beacon of insight and understanding. At any stage, whatever my capacities, Freud has represented for me the possibility of an opening to what can be known at the deepest level. Tonight, I would like to speak about how I encounter Freud now, at this juncture of my life, and to use this opportunity to describe some of what in his work I find most interesting currently.

I thought I would refer to a few of Freud's texts focusing on the late paper, "Analysis Terminable and Interminable", as places to enter into a discussion of my experience of Freud. "Analysis Terminable and Interminable" is also a good foil for the theme of taking stock of Freud's system of thought, a system that clearly represents a discovery. Much as we are taking stock this evening of Freud's influence on us, Freud does so in this paper: a great thinker looking over the work and the practice his path of inquiry has led him to.

Published in 1937 shortly after he had turned 81, Freud begins "Analysis Terminable and Interminable" by examining the question of whether and how an analysis could be shortened. To approach this question, he brings together the many factors he has advanced through the development of his theory that, for him, constitute the experience of the human subject. For Freud these factors also demarcate ongoing moments of engagement of the subject in the world, moments that the individual must negotiate and that create the potential for the most significant pitfalls. Therefore, they inevitably will be present in any analysis.

These factors include the experience of trauma; the drives—here, he particularly focuses on the death drive that for some patients will manifest as masochism and in the treatment as a negative therapeutic reaction; the ego's attempts to defend against the drive and its consequent deformation; the conscious experience of not knowing and not wanting to know that Freud likens to the censoring of a hidden text that operates and remains extant in the unconscious; and the castration complex and its differential effects on males and females that form the problematics of sexual difference.

Importantly, Freud also takes up the question of an individual's need—and he includes the analyst's—to return to analytic work given the experience of these phenomena and the way in which the pressures of life, or for the analyst, the power of analytic work, keeps them mobile. In this regard, Freud brings up examples of unresolved transference from his treatment of Ferenczi and of the postanalytic emergence of a latent masochism in one of his female patients that serves to disguise the later life experience of a forbidden desire. Freud's message about the difficulty of protecting earlier therapeutic gains is made to the analysts of his day but could be to all of us as well. The ongoing pressures of life as well as those we encounter in our work require us to continually reshape our positions—both psychological and ethical—in relation to two of the key problems posed by the Oedipus complex: sexuality and the pressures of a perverse drive; and the challenges entailed—not just for Hamlet—in the murder of the father.

Given the complexity of these issues, we can understand how, from the outset, Freud is skeptical of the possibility of a time-limited analysis. Yes, analysis is 'a time consuming business,' and shortening the process would meet the requirements of expediency, and even, he adds, of American prosperity. But as for the efforts to do so he remarks, "there was probably still at work in them…some trace of the impatient contempt with which the medical science of an earlier day regarded the neuroses as being uncalled-for consequences of invisible injuries" (Freud 1937:216).

Normative science might be contemptuous of the invisible injuries of the neurotic. Yet, confronting the individual in its radiating effects, the un-seen, something outside of perception is what Freud immediately turns to as posing an obstacle to a more expedient treatment. This is not surprising and I would like to spend a little time on this issue. The idea of the invisible injury, something forgotten that works silently, as it were, but that can be discerned in the symptom, in repetition, the dream, or key elements in the patient's discourse that disrupt a settled façade of narrative was one of the hallmarks of Freud's discovery and his theory from the outset. But by the time of his writing "Analysis Terminable and Interminable", Freud had worked out a more complex theory of the invisible and the prevalence in the unconscious of the purely mental object, an object not linked to a neurophysiological correlate. Here, I am not, of course, thinking of an object relation. A mental object could be, for instance, a privileged unconscious fantasy that guides the patient or the lasting effects of the uncanny, a chimera representing the unconscious encounter with the phenomenon of castration. Over time, the invisible injury for Freud became the variety of potentially destabilizing mental objects that the individual is required to negotiate or defend against. Importantly, however, these mental objects for Freud occur at places of vacillation between what is representable and non-representable. They, therefore, create the human experience as coming together across a series of gaps and disjunctions, implied or latent spaces that insist on representation. The human experience for Freud becomes an experience of struggle across a profound divide.

One of the moments, metapsychologically speaking, that creates this divide in the human being and that remains active as trauma, mental object and insistent space, is figured in Freud's model of hallucinatory wish-fulfillment. In this model, the infant seeks to regain the

experience of pleasurable wholeness with the mother, only
to be confronted by the mediation of a mental representation, the hallucination. This mediation that even at this
earliest juncture implies the nascent presence of the father
and the latent system of signification, creates in the child
something peculiarly human, the presence of a forever-lost
object. It becomes one of the problems, perhaps the problem par excellence, of being human.

Freud implicitly takes up this problem next in the paper. Referring to Rank's 1924 paper, "The Trauma of
Birth", Freud looks at the possibility of directly addressing
the patient's primal fixation to the lost object. But he dis-
misses this possibility using a well-known simile, likening
this kind of primal therapy to the fire brigade that enters a
blazing house and intervenes by removing the lamp that
set it off. For Freud, the presence of a lost object, present
outside of representation, nevertheless insisting on representation explains conditions that set the entire being on
fire. This peculiar presence introduces into the drive the
status of a function on the border of the somatic and psychic. And it introduces a precariousness into the emergence of desire given the individual's need to defend
against the drive.

Freud moved away from the seduction theory because he wanted to find more fundamental causes of the
problem of being human. He wanted to investigate the
problem of being human at its limits, an investigation that
as Willi Appolon in Quebec articulates, took Freud outside
of the limits of perception and space and time. Freud
wanted to push his investigation towards what he often
called and does so in this paper, the level of ultimate
things and these came to include, to reference Appolon
again, a central object of psychoanalysis, the unconscious
fantasy. While these things have connections to the biological, anatomical or perceptual, it is the continual evoca-
tion of a mental object outside of and in between these
parameters that creates the human. The body is involved
but not at the level of function. The Wolf Man's fantasy of

being born of his father, for instance, is connected to the body but has lost its connection to the biological.

Consider also the following. In his 1919 paper, "'A Child Is Being Beaten': A Contribution to the Study of the Origin of Sexual Perversions", Freud describes the successive stages of a beating fantasy. The first and third phases, where the beating is being done to another child, are discernible as they enter consciousness. But of the second phase, the stage of fantasy in which the child herself is beaten and derives erotic pleasure from it, Freud says, "This second phase is the most important and the most momentous of all. But we may say of it in a certain sense that it has never had a real existence. It is never remembered; it has never succeeded in becoming conscious. It is a construction of analysis, but it is no less a necessity on that account" (Freud 1919:185).

Here, Freud suggests that psychoanalysis through construction and not memory has given status to a new category of mental object. This object is born of the possibility that analysis gives to establish a place for the unconscious to speak and to be heard.

Where do we find other such instances in Freud that create the human out of a point of vacillation between the non-representable and the insistent need for representation? I think we find them in the configuration of the navel of the dream; the establishment of signification out of the first symbolization of the mother as presence and absence in the child's fort-da game; in the notion of the ternary system of subjective experience instituted through the law and the prohibition of incest by the dead father.

For Freud, the human subject must acquire the privileges and status of being a full subject by negotiating these mental objects in new ways. The subject must, he says in "Analysis Terminable and Interminable", replace "by a correct solution the inadequate decision made in his early life" (Freud 1937:220). Freud was focused on the freedom of the subject from the time he put forward in the *Studies on Hysteria* the idea of a subject who is liberated through speech.

But if Freud established a new status of the mental object, it would seem that at the end of his work, the status of the subject has been transformed as well. In "Analysis Terminable and Interminable", he asks "Is it not precisely the claim of our theory that analysis produces a state which never does arise spontaneously in the ego and that this newly created state constitutes the essential difference between a person who has been analyzed and a person who has not (Freud 1937:227)?"

To become a full subject, the individual must want to know about her or his decisions in relation to the invisible and non-representable mental object. Taking this position, the subject is beset by a fever of wanting to know. This, in my mind, begins to describe the experience of clinical work that unfolds in the framework of the Freudian system.

I have experienced the delight and thrill of pursuing knowledge through the pathways forged by Freud and his great reader, Lacan. Lacan furthered the understanding of the human subject begun by Freud. As with any major pursuit in life, it has not been a simple or easy project but it has been filled with creative moments.

Last year I was speaking to Cordelia (Schmidt-Hellerau) at the beginning of a meeting of the metapsychology workshop. Having finished her teaching of one of the Freud courses, she asked me how the one I was teaching was going. I mentioned that I had just finished re-reading the Wolf Man case and was taken by surprise at how new it seemed to me, although I had read it many times before. Reflecting on this experience, I thought about how knowledge is a continual process of configuring, transforming, dismantling and reconfiguring punctuated by the creative effects of metaphor and genius. Knowledge does go beyond pleasure. The Wolf Man case, I think, is a good place to begin a celebration of Freud's work. There is a convergence here in Freud's wanting to know about the Wolf Man to the limit and thus to acquire

psychoanalytic knowledge at the limit, and our own wanting to follow Freud's path of developing knowledge as a
way of pursuing knowing for ourselves, our own path of
knowledge. I always find it powerful to recall Freud's almost elegiac statement on knowledge that he makes at the
beginning of the Wolf Man case: "Only in such cases," he
writes, "do we succeed in descending into the deepest and
most primitive strata of mental development....And we
feel afterwards that, strictly speaking, only an analysis that
has penetrated so far deserves the name. Naturally a single
case does not give us all the information that we should
like to have. Or, to put it more correctly, it might teach us
everything, if we were only in a position to make everything out, and if we were not compelled by the inexperi-
ence of our own perception to content ourselves with a
little" (Freud 1918[1914]:10).

References

Freud, S. (1918[1914])   From the History of an Infantile
    Neurosis. *Standard Edition*, Volume 17.
Freud, S. (1919) 'A Child is Being Beaten': A Contribution
    to the Study of the Origin of Sexual Perversions. *Stan-
    dard Edition*, Volume 17.
Freud, S. (1937)   Analysis Terminable and Interminable.
    Standard Edition, Volume 23.

www.ingramcontent.com/pod-product-compliance
Lightning Source LLC
Chambersburg PA
CBHW070438290526
45791CB00005B/2027